BEAT-THE-CLOCK
P**UZZLES

BEAT-THE-CLOCK

P ZZLES

FRASER SIMPSON

STERLING PUBLISHING CO., INC.

NEW YORK

2 4 6 8 10 9 7 5 3

Published in 2005 by Sterling Publishing Co., Inc.
387 Park Avenue South, New York, NY 10016

Copyright © 2005 by Fraser Simpson

Distributed in Canada by Sterling Publishing
c/o Canadian Manda Group, 165 Dufferin Street,
Toronto, Ontario, Canada M6K 3H6
Distributed in Great Britain by Chrysalis Books Group PLC
The Chrysalis Building, Bramley Road, London W10 6SP, England
Distributed in Australia by Capricorn Link (Australia) Pty. Ltd.
P.O. Box 704, Windsor, NSW 2756, Australia

Manufactured in the United States of America
All rights reserved

Sterling ISBN 1-4027-1783-0

For information about custom editions, special sales, premium and
corporate purchases, please contact Sterling Special Sales
Department at 800-805-5489 or specialsales@sterlingpub.com.

CONTENTS

50/50 TRIVIA QUIZ 1

 Here's a little warm-up to get your brain ready for the workout it's going to receive from the following puzzles. For each statement circle the correct word from the two below it. You have exactly one (1) minute to read and answer the following questions. You need a pencil and the stopwatch to do this quiz. When the three minutes are up, stop working, whether or not you're finished. Ready, set, go!

1. Color of New England clam chowder
   red   white
2. Last letter of the Greek alphabet
   omega   zeta
3. SAT maximum score
   1600   1800
4. Alopecia involves losing this
   eyesight   hair
5. Ore that provides aluminum
   bauxite   cassiterite
6. Chesspiece with a slit in its head
   bishop   pawn
7. Number of atria in the human heart
   2   4
8. Author of *Emma*
   Austen   Brontë
9. First aviator to fly solo around the world
   Lindbergh   Post
10. French word for Friday
    jeudi   *vendredi*

ANAGRAM QUIZ 1

Match each capitalized anagram with the definition of the anagram by writing the appropriate capital letter in the blank. For example, you would match the anagram ARCHES with the definition "Hunt," since ARCHES rearranges into SEARCH, which fits the definition. You have exactly ten (10) minutes to read and match all four groups. If you finish early, give yourself an extra point for every full minute early that you finished. You need a pencil and the stopwatch to do this quiz. Ready, set, go!

Group One

A	Foaming at the mouth	_____	BINDER
B	Safe to swallow	_____	PALM
C	Deli "doughnut"	_____	BELIED
D	Bedside table item	_____	CHAIN
E	Home storage space	_____	BRAID
F	Dishes	_____	GABLE
G	Instinctive	_____	TACIT

Group Two

A	Striped beast	_____	DEBUTS
B	Parisian eatery	_____	BRAZE
C	Calendar month	_____	ACRES
D	Not difficult	_____	ORBITS
E	Say "Boo!" to	_____	AYES
F	Arrested (slang)	_____	SWEAT
G	Squander	_____	CHARM

Group Three

A	Gave an under-the-table incentive	_____	ADDER
B	Pasta go-with	_____	CLERIC
C	Round shape	_____	ARCED
D	Royal proclamation	_____	WHAT
E	Overwhelming fear	_____	CAUSE
F	Moth-repelling wood	_____	RECEDE
G	Springtime event	_____	RIBBED

Group Four

A	Couch	_____	OCCURS
B	Flower of early spring	_____	GROAN
C	The Charleston, e.g.	_____	LEASE
D	Non-speaking movie character	_____	OAFS
E	Cereal dish	_____	CANED
F	Fluorescent lamp gas	_____	BLOW
G	Stand for art	_____	TAXER

THINK FAST QUIZ 1

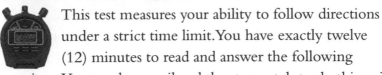

This test measures your ability to follow directions under a strict time limit. You have exactly twelve (12) minutes to read and answer the following questions. You need a pencil and the stopwatch to do this quiz. When the twelve minutes are up, stop working, whether or not you're finished. Ready, set, go!

The number of times letter A makes an appearance in this particular sentence is _____. Ignore the next sentence, unless December comes right before January. How many days are in December and January combined? _____. Assume that no winged creature needs to eat and no fish have wings. Can it be concluded that no fish needs to eat? Yes or no: _____. In the diagram at the right, some cubes are stacked in the corner of a room. How many cubes are there? _____. If you think a cat swims well, write SWIMS in capital letters in this blank: _____. Otherwise, write it up-side-down in the blank. What word can precede BOARD, FISH, GAZING, and STRUCK? _____. Pay no attention to the next sentence unless an elephant has tires or a car has a trunk. If the previous sentence has an even number of words, leave this space blank: _____. If it doesn't, write ODD instead. If Paul gives Barb three times as many candies as he gives Sal, and gives Sal 10 fewer candies than he gives Barb, how many candies does Sal get? _____.

Figure out how to read the message below and write the 7-letter item it describes: _____.

H	E	N	A	P	P
C	C	O	O	K	L
T	T	A	D	S	I
I	A	E	R	B	A
K	H	T	E	C	N

In this space _____ write the next letter alphabetically after N that has no curves when written in block capitals, unless that letter is W, in which case leave it blank. Circle the odd one out: ACELM, ABERZ, ABILY, EGIRT. Think of five 5-letter uncapitalized English words that begin with B and end with K:

_____ _____ _____ _____

_____. If torture isn't agonizing, write TORTURE here: _____. Otherwise, write only the four letters in the odd positions of that word. In the figure below, circle the circle that is three clockwise from the circle opposite the circle that is two counter-clockwise from the circle containing the number 4. Write FOE in this blank _____ unless this is the last sentence, in which case write the result of shifting each letter of FOE back one position in the alphabet.

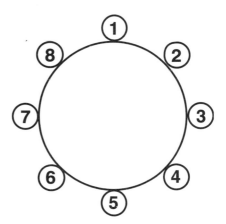

50/50 TRIVIA QUIZ 2

For each statement circle the correct word from the two below it. You have exactly three (3) minutes to read and answer the following questions. When the three minutes are up, stop working. Ready, set, go!

1. William Tell's country
   England   Switzerland

2. Study of insects
   entomology   etymology

3. Zodiac sign of those born on February 29
   Pisces   Aries

4. Age that followed the Stone Age
   Bronze   Iron

5. State containing Auburn University
   Alabama   Mississippi

6. Marie Antoinette's country of birth
   Austria   Germany

7. "The Man of a Thousand Faces"
   Chaney   Lugosi

8. Human body's longest bone
   tibia   femur

9. Number of faces on an icosahedron
   20   24

10. Capital of Iran
    Tehran   Baghdad

11. Amount of time Noah was afloat
    40 days   7 months

12. Largest Mediterranean island
    Cyprus   Sicily

13. McCarthyism decade
    1950s   1960s

14. Country from which we get the Doberman
    Germany   Austria

15. Author of *Crime and Punishment*
    Dostoyevsky   Tolstoy

16. Slob in *The Odd Couple*
    Felix   Oscar

17. Artist who painted *The Last Supper*
    Michelangelo   da Vinci

18. Russian for "openness"
    glasnost   *perestroika*

19. Number of players on a basketball team
    5   6

20. Last word of the film *Gone With the Wind*
    damn   day

LETTER INSERTION QUIZ 1

Insert a letter into each capitalized word to form a new word, and match the result with a definition on the right. Write the added letter in the blank beside the definition. For example, given CURSE, you can insert O to make COURSE and then write the letter O in the blank beside the definition "School offering." As a bonus, the filled blanks in each grouping spell a common English word. You have exactly ten (10) minutes to match all five groups. If you finish early, give yourself an extra point for every full minute early that you finished. You need a pencil and the stopwatch to do this quiz. Ready, set, go!

Group One

SHRED   _____ Flour or sugar

SURLY   _____ Doubtless

STALE   _____ Mentally sharp

Group Two

CASTE   _____ Vigorous

DETER   _____ Weight watcher

PARTY   _____ Prince's home

ROUST   _____ Somewhat

Group Three

CATER   _____ Squelch

GROVE   _____ Lunar depression

MONEY   _____ Place for a phonograph needle

PLAID   _____ Unruffled

STILE   _____ Mischievous child

Group Four

COMIC	_____	Hurt
DEUCE	_____	Hate
INURE	_____	Of the universe
LATHE	_____	Having more cash
RICER	_____	Seamstress's activity
SWING	_____	Reason out

Group Five

BRIDE	_____	Prince's home
DRESS	_____	Coercion
DRIVE	_____	River crosser
FRIED	_____	Restorative medication
GUESS	_____	Reason out
PLACE	_____	Pal
REEDY	_____	Party invitees

THINK FAST QUIZ 2

 This test measures your ability to follow directions under a strict time limit. You have exactly fifteen (15) minutes to read and answer the following questions. You need a pencil and the stopwatch to do this quiz. When the fifteen minutes are up, stop working, whether or not you're finished. Ready, set, go!

The letter that occurs least often (although at least once) in this sentence of the test is _____. Write the letters Z, Y, X, W, V in backward order here: ___ ___ ___ ___ ___. If fish don't have wings, write BIRD in this space: _____. Otherwise, leave it blank. How many triangles (of any size) are in diagram at right? _____. Read this sentence by placing W at the front of each group of letters and then answer in the space provided: rite hat ord eds "ay" ith "ard" _____. What number, multiplied by 2, becomes one-fifth of 100? _____. Think of five world countries whose names begin with the letter I: _____ _____ _____ _____ _____. In the diagram below, cross out three toothpicks to leave three squares, unless that would leave 10 toothpicks, in which case cross out only one toothpick to leave three squares.

16

If GANGLIONS = 123456789, what word is 968425731? _____. Underline the only word among these five that contains all five vowels: reduction, marvelous, cowardice, equation, subinterval. Leave this space blank _____ unless April is five months before October, in which case write MONTH in the space. In their pencil cases, Meg has twice as many pencils as Peg, and Peg has twice as many pencils as Reg. If Meg has three more pencils than Peg and Reg together, how many pencils has Meg? _____. In the grid below, write a B in the square to the right of the U, unless B is not the last letter of rhubarb, in which case write a D instead. Write a Y one square below the square two to the right of the P. Write an R in the square directly to the left of the square directly to the right of the square diagonally adjacent to the Y. Then finish filling in the grid so that six common words are formed across and down. Assume that people are either crass or polite but not both, and that all crass people wear scarves and all polite people wear hats. Can it be concluded that no person wears both a scarf and a hat? Yes or no: _____. If you can't anagram the letters of NODE to make another word, write NONE; otherwise, write the anagram: _____.

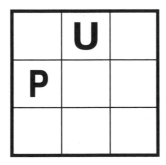

BRAIN STRETCHERS QUIZ 1

Match each item on the left with one on the right by writing the appropriate capital letter in the blank. The matches are based on similar meanings, but watch out for tricky wordplay including double meanings and altered spacing within words. For example, you would match "anti-diplomacy" with "contact" (con tact). You have exactly twenty (20) minutes to read and match all five groups. If you finish early, give yourself an extra point for every full minute early that you finished. You need a pencil and the stopwatch to do this quiz. Ready, set, go!

Group One

A	Goat	_____	Dress down
B	Preen	_____	"You must be this tall to ride"
C	Fair warning	_____	Past tense
D	Number 8	_____	Butter
E	Overanxious	_____	Blackball

Group Two

A	Goat	_____	Nightmare
B	Passenger	_____	Get ready to stoke
C	Sympathy pains	_____	Trainee
D	Dark horse	_____	Coaches
E	Draw poker	_____	Attack

Group Three

A	Fashion plates	_____	Retired journalists
B	Drove crazy	_____	Dentists
C	Express	_____	Make pottery
D	Body shop	_____	Benched rowers
E	Crew cuts	_____	Mad cows

Group Four

A	Engagement ring	_____	Dope fiend
B	Honeysuckle bush	_____	Boxing arena
C	Moorages	_____	Ramparts
D	Horns, wool	_____	Elder cousin
E	News junkie	_____	Mad cows

Group Five

A	Dog race	_____	Depressing
B	Wrinkling	_____	Parchment
C	Triplets	_____	Regattas
D	Current events	_____	Jaunts
E	Thirst	_____	Say the dinner blessing

THINK FAST QUIZ 3

This test measures your ability to follow directions under a strict time limit. You have exactly twenty (20) minutes to read and answer the following questions. You need a pencil and the stopwatch to do this quiz. When the twenty minutes are up, stop working, whether or not you're finished. Ready, set, go!

Shift the letters TUBSU one position back in the alphabet: _____. Circle the sixth occurrence of the letter C in this sentence. If lemons aren't sweet, write LIMES in this space _____, but if ripe strawberries aren't red, enter GREEN here _____. Divide the shape to theright along the lines to make two identical pieces with the same orientation. What four-letter word can be placed in front of each of the words CHAIR, GOING, MONEY, RIDER, and STREET to form five familiar compound words or phrases? _____. What word can precede BAND, CEMENT, GLOVES and NECK? _____. Ignore the next sentence unless clubs and spades are red suits. Write an X in this space: _____. If there are any repeated letters in the word ambidextrously, write RIGHT;otherwise, write LEFT _____.

Figure out the pattern in the diagram below and draw what should go in the blank square. Assume that some stage plays are not amusing and that I enjoy anything amusing. Can it be concluded that there are some stage plays that I do not enjoy? Yes or no: _____. Circle the word that does not sound like another word when you lisp it: symbol, gross, faceful, unsinkable, basset. Don is four times as old as his brother Jon. If Don is 16 now, at what age will Don be twice as old as Jon? _____. Name five animals that start with the letter H: _____ _____ _____ _____ _____. In the grid below, put a box around the only 3x3 square that contains 9 different digits.

```
7  8  3  9  2  8  1  3
6  5  2  8  5  6  7  2
3  1  4  7  1  4  5  6
5  2  9  6  2  9  3  1
7  8  1  5  3  7  4  2
9  4  3  7  8  1  5  8
1  2  5  1  2  9  4  6
4  6  7  4  6  3  2  1
```

Build a six-letter word by putting the opposite of OUT inside what a trout is, and write the result here: _____.

50/50 TRIVIA QUIZ 3

 For each statement circle the correct word from the two below it. You have exactly three (3) minutes to read and answer the following questions. When the three minutes are up, stop working. Ready, set, go!

1. Most frequently used consonant in English
   S   T

2. Fossilized tree resin used in jewelry
   amber   jade

3. City containing the Anne Frank House
   Amsterdam   Berlin

4. Sir Alexander Fleming's discovery
   insulin   penicillin

5. Bandleader who wrote "Moonlight Serenade"
   Miller   Welk

6. Capital of Pakistan
   Islamabad   Kirachi

7. Main ingredient of Coquilles St. Jacques
   oysters   scallops

8. Author of *This Side of Paradise*
   Faulkner   Fitzgerald

9. Term for a group of foxes
   clowder   skulk

10. Date of Bastille Day
    June 14   July 14

11. The Gopher State
    Delaware   Minnesota

12. World War featuring The Battle of the Bulge
    First   Second

13. Planet with a mountain called Olympus Mons
    Mercury   Mars

14. Civilization that had its capital at Cuzco
    Incan   Mayan

15. Artist who painted *The Potato Eaters*
    Manet   Van Gogh

16. Angle classification between 90° and 180°
    acute   obtuse

17. Medical term for the upper jaw
    maxilla   mandible

18. Mythological figure who slew Medusa
    Perseus   Theseus

19. France's longest river
    Loire   Seine

20. What a cooper makes
    barrels   shoes

50/50 TRIVIA QUIZ 4

For each statement circle the correct word from the two below it. You have exactly three (3) minutes to read and answer the following questions. When the three minutes are up, stop working. Ready, set, go!

1. Alexander the Great's land

   Greece   Macedonia

2. Tin Man's lack, in *The Wizard of Oz*

   brain   heart

3. Country with a solid green flag

   Libya   Kenya

4. Planet with a moon called Titan

   Jupiter   Saturn

5. War featuring The Battle of New Orleans

   Civil War   War of 1812

6. Columbus Day's month

   September   October

7. Term for a young otter

   kitten   pup

8. Artist who painted *The Night Watch*

   Rembrandt   Van Gogh

9. Color-sensitive retina cell

   rod   cone

10. What "Stalin" means
    saint   steel

11. Ringo replaced this Beatles drummer
    Best   Sutcliffe

12. "Singing in the Rain" singer
    Astaire   Kelly

13. Year in which the French Revolution began
    1789   1791

14. Element that makes stainless steel "stainless"
    chromium   zinc

15. Body part used to tell the age of a horse
    teeth   mane

16. Country containing Mecca
    Saudi Arabia   Yemen

17. Number of zeros in one trillion
    9   12

18. Author of *The Time Machine*
    Orwell   Wells

19. Language of origin of the word "balcony"
    Italian   Spanish

20. How long Robinson Crusoe was a castaway
    14 years   28 years

SCRAMBLE UP QUIZ 1

Insert a letter into each capitalized word and then rearrange these letters to form a new word. Match the result with a definition on the right. Write the added letter in the blank beside the definition. For example, given ONION, you can insert T and rearrange to make NOTION and then write the letter T in the blank beside the definition "Thought." As a bonus, the filled blanks in each grouping spell a common English word. You have exactly fifteen (15) minutes to match all five groups. If you finish early, give yourself an extra point for every full minute early that you finished. You need a pencil and the stopwatch to do this quiz. Ready, set, go!

Group One

BREAD	_____	On stage
DEMON	_____	*The Thinker*, for one
GIANT	_____	Thoroughly up-to-date
MAULS	_____	Word often ending in –ly
TASTE	_____	Sanctuary

Group Two

DREAM	_____	Floating aimlessly
EARLY	_____	Look up to
EDICT	_____	Sock pattern
LATER	_____	Provoked scratching
TRIAD	_____	Baby's noisy toy

Group Three

LUTES	_____	Ski lodge
AMISS	_____	Marzipan nut
LATCH	_____	Not obvious
NOMAD	_____	Sentence ending
PRIDE	_____	Hindu wise men

Group Four

AROSE	_____	Read carefully
CHEST	_____	Verdi works
CURSE	_____	Cause of a rash, sometimes
PRIDE	_____	Really bad smell
RUPEE	_____	Lollipop

Group Five

YEAST	_____	Maiden "in distress"
TARRY	_____	Pat on the back
SPEAR	_____	Mass departure
LEADS	_____	Aorta, for example
DOUSE	_____	High school sweetheart

THINK FAST QUIZ 4

 This test measures your ability to follow directions under a strict time limit. You have exactly twenty (20) minutes to read and answer the following questions. You need a pencil and the stopwatch to do this quiz. When the twenty minutes are up, stop working, whether or not you're finished. Ready, set, go!

Cross off the forty-fifth letter of this sentence, not counting Fs. Now cross off the fifth letter in this sentence, counting only Fs. Write SNAP & STOP in reverse order in this space: _____. If rum is not alcoholic, shift each letter of RUM back six places in the alphabet and write the result here: _____. Otherwise, shift each of the letters of the word RUM forward two places in the alphabet and write the result here: _____. How many rectangles (of any size) are in the diagram at the right?_____. Underline the word that doesn't contain a hidden bird: contravene, probing, microwave, expandable, Lawrence. Ignore every third word in the following instruction: If limes carrots are green purple, write three four Xs above under this line: _____. Assume that no ogres are truly ugly and that some truly ugly things are horrifying. Can it be concluded that some horrifying things are not ogres? Yes or no: _____.

28

In the face down cards in the diagram below, a seven lies to the left of a three, a spade to the right of a diamond, a heart to the left of a king, and a three to the right of a king. Name the three cards in order from left to right: _____ _____ _____.

What number, multiplied by 2, becomes ⁴/₅ of 40 _____? Put a box around the only word that doesn't consist solely of letters from the second half of the alphabet: proxy, worst, prowl, yours, rusty, sport. Name two chemical elements that begin with S but do not end with M: _____ _____.
The piece of paper to the right is divided into 16 sections.
Imagine laying the paper on a table. Fold the paper in half by bringing the left edge over to the right; in half again by bringing the bottom edge up to the top; again by bringing the left edge over to the right; and once more, bringing the bottom edge up. Which numbered section is

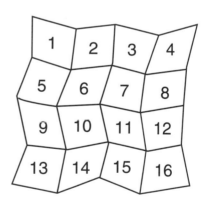

now on top? _____. What letter can be put at the front of each of the following words to make four new words: ASHES, ELVES, LIGHT, OLDER? _____. If SO doesn't sound like SEW, then write QUITE in this blank: _____.
Otherwise, just write the first four letters of that word.

ANAGRAM QUIZ 2

Match each capitalized anagram with the definition of the anagram by writing the appropriate capital letter in the blank. For example, you would match the anagram ARCHES with the definition "Hunt," since ARCHES rearranges into SEARCH, which fits the definition. You have exactly twelve (12) minutes to read and match all four groups. If you finish early, give yourself an extra point for every full minute early that you finished. You need a pencil and the stopwatch to do this quiz. Ready, set, go!

Group One

A Match in opinion   _____ SAGES
B Not as dangerous   _____ ARTY
C Plus-sized   _____ EAGER
D Indicate a turn   _____ GLARE
E Tea set platter   _____ SATING
F Huge people   _____ FEARS
G Helium, nitrogen, et al. _____ ALIGNS

Group Two

A Test answer   _____ GLEAN
B Bridge bid   _____ OARED
C Gabriel, e.g.   _____ ANOINT
D Country   _____ ASPS
E Soda flavor   _____ FLEAS
F Painter or musician   _____ PAGER
G Really fancy   _____ STRAIT

Group Three

A	Dog's controller	_____	APRONS
B	Dog's wagger	_____	UNWARY
C	Troubled feeling	_____	ALIT
D	Sermon deliverer	_____	AMONG
E	Tropical fruit	_____	GNATS
F	Landing strip	_____	MYNA
G	A lot	_____	SHALE

Group Four

A	Ruins	_____	LAST
B	Bad blood	_____	BRIDES
C	Blood mover	_____	ALOFT
D	Understated	_____	WAKES
E	Parade entry	_____	BLUEST
F	Common seasoning	_____	EARTH
G	Crooked	_____	RANGE

THINK FAST QUIZ 5

This test measures your ability to follow directions under a strict time limit. You have exactly fifteen (15) minutes to read and answer the following questions. You need a pencil and the stopwatch to do this quiz. When the fifteen minutes are up, stop working, whether or not you're finished. Ready, set, go!

Circle the two vowels in the next sentence that are not Us. Dump trucks mustn't churn up such unusual chunks, but succumb under mud. If ovens aren't used for baking, write CHEF here: _____. How many cubes appear in the stack in the diagram at the right? _____. If LENS = 1234, what word is 4234212443244? _____. If today is Thursday, what day of the week was it 31 days ago?_____.

In the diagram below, make a word ladder than links DIP to OAR, changing only one letter at a time and always having a common word at each step.

D I P

——

——

——

OAR

Read every second letter in the following words and answer the resulting question: Sook wombat nay allergist Dvorak notes ahead view? _____. Assume that no clowns are funny and that none but clowns do juggling. Can it be concluded that no funny people do juggling? Yes or no: _____. What word can precede CREAM, FISHING, PICK, and SKATER? _____. Leave this space blank _____unless there are 12 two-cent stamps in a dozen, in which case write MAIL in the space. Underline the word that does not contain three consecutive letters of the alphabet in reverse order: jihad, redcap, amongst, gutsy, pontoon, songfest. List 5 four-letter words that begin and end with P: _____ _____ _____ _____ _____. My wallet contains eight dollars more than twice the money in your wallet. Looked at another way, my wallet has four times as much money as your wallet. How many dollars are in my wallet? _____. Pay no attention to the next sentence unless pigs have fingers or clocks have hands. Circle the last word in the previous sentence. In the space below, write a three-letter part of a fish that's slang for $5, but only if 20 quarters equals five dollars. Write the word BEER right after it, unless beer is sometimes called suds, in which case write ALE there instead.

50/50 TRIVIA QUIZ 5

 For each statement circle the correct word from the two below it. You have exactly three (3) minutes to read and answer the following questions. When the three minutes are up, stop working. Ready, set, go!

1. Metal that is the best conductor

    gold   silver

2. Abbreviation that means "that is"

    e.g.   i.e.

3. The "Lion of Judah"

    Idi Amin   Haile Selassie

4. Canada's largest province by area

    Ontario   Quebec

5. Religious leader born in 551 B.C.

    Buddha   Confucius

6. Small kangaroo

    wallaby   dingo

7. Artist who painted *The Birth of Venus*

    Botticelli   Tintoretto

8. Roman numeral 19

    XIX   XXI

9. Flag Day in the U.S.

    February   June

10. Thailand's former name
    Ceylon   Siam

11. Disney dwarf who wore glasses
    Bashful   Doc

12. What *Mein Kampf* means
    My Camp   My Struggle

13. "Who steals my purse steals trash" speaker
    Desdemona   Iago

14. Female sex chromosome pair
    XX   XY

15. Second tallest of the 7 Wonders of the Ancient World
    lighthouse   Colossus

16. Composer of the "Trout Quintet"
    Mendelssohn   Schubert

17. Florence Nightingale's birth city
    Florence   Paris

18. Planet that spins the opposite way
    Venus   Uranus

19. What an oologist studies
    bones   eggs

20. Author of *The Pilgrim's Progress*
    Bunyan   Milton

50/50 TRIVIA QUIZ 6

For each statement circle the correct word from the two below it. You have exactly three (3) minutes to read and answer the following questions. When the three minutes are up, stop working. Ready, set, go!

1. What "matriculate" means

   enroll   graduate

2. Roman emperor after Claudius

   Caligula   Nero

3. Author of *The Martian Chronicles*

   Asimov   Bradbury

4. Number of bones in the human body

   206   208

5. Sweeney Todd's profession

   barber   butcher

6. European country whose capital is Vaduz

   Liechenstein   Luxembourg

7. War in which TV's "M★A★S★H" was set

   Korean   Vietnam

8. Composer of *Eugene Onegin*

   Prokofiev   Tchaikovsky

9. Artist who drew the Uncle Sam image

   Flagg   Nast

10. Metal extracted from the ore cinnabar
    mercury   nickel

11. Fifth book of the Old Testament
    Deuteronomy   Numbers

12. Chemical symbol for copper
    Cp   Cu

13. Mammal that lives the longest
    elephant   human

14. Number of pints in a quart
    2   4

15. Groundhog Day
    Feb 2   Feb 3

16. Treaty ending the First World War
    Paris   Versailles

17. Latitude of the North Pole
    90°   180°

18. Planet with the shortest day
    Mercury   Jupiter

19. Number of arms on a squid
    8   10

20. What a deltiologist collects
    matchbooks   postcards

THINK FAST QUIZ 6

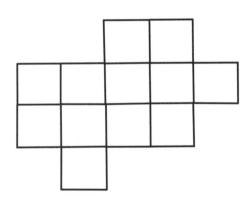

This test measures your ability to follow directions under a strict time limit. You have exactly twelve (12) minutes to read and answer the following questions. You need a pencil and the stopwatch to do this quiz. When the twelve minutes are up, stop working, whether or not you're finished. Ready, set, go!

Write the five letters N, G, E, B, I in alphabetical order: _____. Count the number of Ts in this sentence, and write your total in this blank: _____. Divide the shape below along the lines to make two identical pieces with the same orientation.

Think of a digit. Double it and then add nine. Multiply the result by five. Remove the last digit and subtract your original number. Write your final result here: _____. If ice isn't warm, write HOT here: _____. Remove a different letter from each of these words to make an arithmetic question and then write the answer: thirsty plush flour _____. List three countries that begin with M and end with O: _____

_____ _____. Assume that all who want to succeed study economics, and that some lawyers study economics. Can it be concluded that some lawyers want to succeed? Yes or no: _____. What word can precede CLEANER, DREAM, LINE, and ORGAN? _____. In the calendar below, cross out these three days: first Monday, the last Thursday before the fifth Tuesday, and the second Friday after the last Monday before the third Wednesday.

S	M	T	W	T	F	S
		1	2	3	4	5
6	7	8	9	10	11	12
13	14	15	16	17	18	19
20	21	22	23	24	25	26
27	28	29	30			

If FATHER = 123456, what word is 3456521356? _____. Twenty people are in three rooms marked A, B, and C. Room A contains 3 people, and Room B contains the same number of people as in Rooms A and C combined. How many people are in Room C? ____. Leave this space blank _____ unless plumbers often own steamships or carpenters often own planes, in which case write LEVEL in the space. Don't write BALLOON in this blank _____ unless the word balloon has two pairs of double letters. If you thought this quiz was tricky, write STOP in this blank: _____. Otherwise, write POTS in reverse order in the blank.

50/50 TRIVIA QUIZ 7

For each statement circle the correct word from the two below it. You have exactly three (3) minutes to read and answer the following questions. When the three minutes are up, stop working. Ready, set, go!

1. Chemical symbol for iron
   Fe   Ir

2. Rabies vaccine developer
   Jenner   Pasteur

3. What "largo" means in music
   lively   slowly

4. Sea containing the Isle of Man
   Irish Sea   North Sea

5. Patron saint of hopeless causes
   St. Jude   St. Sebastian

6. How frogs breathe underwater
   gills   skin

7. Artist famous for ballet scenes
   Degas   Monet

8. Unit of resistance in electricity
   ampere   ohm

9. City with an airport called Love Field
   Dallas   Houston

10. Carl Jung's country of birth
    Austria   Switzerland

11. Spanish for "butterfly"
    mariposa   *mimosa*

12. Number of locks in the Suez Canal
    zero   100

13. Author James ____ who wrote *Lost Horizon*
    Clavell   Hilton

14. Planet whose orbit is closest to Earth's
    Venus   Mars

15. Continent with the ruins of Carthage
    Africa   Asia

16. Number of sides that a heptagon has
    6   7

17. Fastest land mammal
    antelope   cheetah

18. Composer of the "Minute Waltz"
    Beethoven   Chopin

19. Medical term for the shoulder blade
    clavicle   scapula

20. Language of origin of the word "brandy"
    French   Dutch

BRAIN STRETCHERS QUIZ 2

Match each item on the left with one on the right by writing the appropriate capital letter in the blank. The matches are based on similar meanings, but watch out for tricky wordplay including double meanings and altered spacing within words. For example, you would match "anti-diplomacy" with "contact" (con tact). You have exactly eighteen (18) minutes to read and match all five groups. If you finish early, give yourself an extra point for every full minute early that you finished. You need a pencil and the stopwatch to do this quiz. Ready, set, go!

Group One

A	Drive shaft	_____	Punctual
B	Bishop	_____	High post
C	Prelate	_____	Golf club
D	Letter opener	_____	Unisex store
E	Air mail	_____	Addressee

Group Two

A	Double feature	_____	Retreat
B	Fortresses	_____	Four eyes
C	Mafia boss	_____	Meeting points
D	Pay again	_____	Sinking
E	Agenda	_____	Like barrettes

42

Group Three

A	Telltale target	_____	Devilry
B	Antibody	_____	Grateful
C	Drumsticks	_____	Spiritual
D	Ashes	_____	Apple
E	Impaction	_____	Brake trouble

Group Four

A	Strong suit	_____	Astronomer
B	Night watchman	_____	Scheming fellow
C	Plangent	_____	Instance
D	Posed	_____	Bible
E	Job holder	_____	Chain mail

Group Five

A	Raisin	_____	Calf
B	Jenny	_____	Sun god's home
C	New Jersey	_____	Imprison
D	Heart specialist	_____	Assess
E	Deliberate	_____	Cupid

THINK FAST QUIZ 7

 This test measures your ability to follow directions under a strict time limit. You have exactly fifteen (15) minutes to read and answer the following questions. You need a pencil and the stopwatch to do this quiz. When the fifteen minutes are up, stop working, whether or not you're finished. Ready, set, go!

Count the number of Es in the next sentence and write your answer here: _____. Whenever even-tempered gentlemen seek revenge, we never sleep. Then rearrange the letters SAIDM to form a mythological king: _____. If the initial letters of "have a nice day" spell a body part, write the initial letters of "five out of ten" here: _____. The time shown by the clock at the right is 4:37. Approximately what time would it be if the hour and minute hands were reversed? _____. Don't write COW in this blank _____ unless milk is green or dogs go "moo." Calculate the sum of the numbers hidden in the words: corniness, network, heighten, auctioned, and acuteness: _____. Assume that all non-terriers are happy and that dogs are all terriers. Must it be true that no dogs are happy? _____.

Figure out how to read the message in the diagram below and write the 8-letter object it describes: _____.

AND	ANI	ATR	HTU
MAL	SKS	UNK	WIT

If 01 = A, 02 = B, 03 = C, and so on up to 26 = Z, decode the word 23151804 and write your answer in this blank: _____. What number, divided by 4, becomes $2/3$ of 12? _____. In the diagram below, how many times does the word HID appear in a straight line horizontally, vertically, or diagonally? _____.

H	D	H	H
I	I	I	D
D	D	I	H

If two-thirds of my book collection is 18 books, how many books do I own? _____. In an alphabetical list, which month comes last? _____. Ignore the next sentence unless the sixth letter of the alphabet is G. Write the seventh letter of the alphabet here: _____. Write the word COMPETE in this blank, leaving a small space after the P _____, and then fill the space with an L.

SCRAMBLE UP QUIZ 2

Insert a letter into each capitalized word and then rearrange these letters to form a new word. Then match the result with a definition on the right. Write the added letter in the blank beside the definition. For example, given ONION, you can insert T and rearrange to make NOTION and then write the letter T in the blank beside the definition "Thought." As a bonus, the filled blanks in each grouping spell a common English word. You have exactly fifteen (15) minutes to match all five groups. If you finish early, give yourself an extra point for every full minute early that you finished. You need a pencil and the stopwatch to do this quiz. Ready, set, go!

Group One

THREE	_____	Wood for building
SQUAT	_____	Winter appliance
BLUER	_____	Gets satisfaction from
NOSEY	_____	Immobilize, at a rodeo
EIGHT	_____	Milk amounts

Group Two

START	_____	Mellow
SCORE	_____	Upriver swimmer
ONSET	_____	Rubens, for one
OPENS	_____	World Cup sport
MASON	_____	Expressed orally

Group Three

GRIND	_____	Pounds, as a headache
SHORT	_____	Chewy candy
SINCE	_____	Sneezer's request
SUITE	_____	There are 12 in each foot
TANGO	_____	On the clothesline

Group Four

WARNS	_____	Olden
TEASE	_____	Afternoon nap, in Spain
EBONY	_____	Cutting tools
SKEIN	_____	Reply
ASSET	_____	Upper house

Group Five

MIRTH	_____	Red salad veggie
PANIC	_____	Attorney
RATIO	_____	Solitude-seeker
EARLY	_____	Guy wearing a thimble
HAIRS	_____	Thrill for felines

THINK FAST QUIZ 8

This test measures your ability to follow directions under a strict time limit. You have exactly sixteen (16) minutes to read and answer the following questions. You need a pencil and the stopwatch to do this quiz. When the sixteen minutes are up, stop working, whether or not you're finished. Ready, set, go!

Count the vowels in this sentence and write the total in this blank: _____. If PRICE = 12345, what word is 125431345? _____. If you turn a left-handed glove inside-out, which hand would it fit on: right or left? _____. Give the only letter of the alphabet that does not make an appearance in this exact sentence of the quiz: _____. How many equilateral triangles (of any size) are in the diagram at the right? _____. List three 6-letter words that begin and end with N: _____ _____ _____. Assume that any knight is right and any lady is shady. Hite is a knight and Sadie is shady. Must Hite be right? _____. Must Sadie be a lady? _____. In the array of playing cards at the right, circle the only card that is not part of a pair or three-of-a-kind, unless queens do not outrank kings, in which case circle two cards of the same suit that total 14.

48

In the group of words that follows, underline the two words that are most nearly opposite in meaning: gentle, cool, crazy, minor, nervous. Complete the magic square below so that each square contains a different number from 0 to 15 and the four numbers in each row, column, and long diagonal add up to 30.

	8	11	
13			14
	15	12	
	4		9

What word can precede BROKEN, GUEST, PLANT, and WARMING? _____. Write OFF at the top of this page—Wait! If OFF is the opposite of ON, write ON at the top of the page, unless ON spells another word backward, in which case write YES. If A = 1, B = 2, C = 3, and so on, what is the value of G times Y ? _____. If the day after tomorrow is two days after Friday, what day of the week was it exactly one week before the day before yesterday? _____. What three letters are common to the two words VERANDA and TENFOLD? _____.

50/50 TRIVIA QUIZ 8

For each statement circle the correct word from the two below it. You have exactly three (3) minutes to read and answer the following questions. When the three minutes are up, stop working. Ready, set, go!

1. Language spoken by ancient Romans
   Greek   Latin

2. Planet with greatest average density
   Mercury   Earth

3. "Peaches and cream" vegetable
   beans   corn

4. Chemical symbol for antimony
   Sb   Ti

5. "Silver Ghost" car brand
   Oldsmobile   Rolls-Royce

6. Animal that's literally a "river horse"
   hippopotamus   alligator

7. Country whose flag is not rectangular
   Bangladesh   Nepal

8. Author of *Utopia*
   More   Pope

9. Northernmost of the Florida Keys
   Key Largo   Key West

10. Spanish artist who painted *Crucifixion*
    Dali   Picasso

11. Another name for the thumb
    pollex   hallux

12. Inventor of vulcanized rubber
    Firestone   Goodyear

13. Roman equivalent of the goddess Artemis
    Demeter   Diana

14. Laissez-faire economist
    Galbraith   Keynes

15. Number of seconds in an hour
    360   3600

16. Substance carved when doing scrimshaw
    ivory   whalebone

17. Shakespeare play that opens "Who's there?"
    Hamlet   *Othello*

18. World capital containing the Trevi fountain
    Paris   Rome

19. Dennis the Menace's dog
    Puff   Ruff

20. Country in which Parmesan cheese originated
    Italy   Switzerland

50/50 TRIVIA QUIZ 9

For each statement circle the correct word from the two below it. You have exactly three (3) minutes to read and answer the following questions. When the three minutes are up, stop working. Ready, set, go!

1. Written defamation
   libel   slander

2. Sulphuric acid
   H_2SO_4 HCl

3. What a vexillologist studies
   flags   medals

4. City containing the Hagia Sophia
   Istanbul   Tangier

5. Third wedding anniversary gift
   leather   wood

6. Number of adult human's teeth
   32   36

7. Oldest U.S. university
   Yale   Harvard

8. Paul Bunyan's pet ox
   Babe   Blue

9. War featuring Pork Chop Hill
   Korean   Vietnam

10. Bronze = copper + _____
    tin   zinc

11. Number of Punic Wars
    2   3

12. Color of Indy 500 starting flag
    green   yellow

13. Brontë who wrote *Wuthering Heights*
    Charlotte   Emily

14. Type of bird a widgeon is
    goose   duck

15. Khan visited by Marco Polo
    Genghis   Kublai

16. Beethoven symphony known as "Eroica"
    3rd   5th

17. Planet with a "Great Red Spot"
    Jupiter   Saturn

18. God of mischief in Norse mythology
    Balder   Loki

19. Number of karats in pure gold
    16   24

20. Artist who died in the Marquesas Islands
    Gauguin   Monet

BRAIN STRETCHERS QUIZ 3

Match each item on the left with one on the right by writing the appropriate capital letter in the blank. The matches are based on similar meanings, but watch out for tricky wordplay including double meanings and altered spacing within words. For example, you would match "anti-diplomacy" with "contact" (con tact). You have exactly fifteen (15) minutes to read and match all five groups. If you finish early, give yourself an extra point for every full minute early that you finished. You need a pencil and the stopwatch to do this quiz. Ready, set, go!

Group One

A	Capon		Deep breathing
B	Patron saint of McDonald's	_____	Tuqued
C	Minus	_____	Deliveryman
D	Scuba	_____	Nonplus
E	Obstetrician	_____	Starches

Group Two

A	Plant life		Fin
B	Cross country	_____	Boxer Rebellion
C	Codpiece	_____	Malta
D	Dogfight	_____	Magician
E	Wander	_____	Factory workers

Group Three

A	Cowed	_____	Stadium groundskeeper
B	Diamond cutter	_____	Spider
C	Webster	_____	Dynasty
D	Power line	_____	Have a double marriage
E	Earphones	_____	Private reception

Group Four

A	Cricket pitch	_____	Gasps
B	Patch	_____	High chirping
C	Infirm	_____	Elks
D	Big bucks	_____	Rent control
E	Short pants	_____	Employed

Group Five

A	Determinate	_____	High heel
B	Wave	_____	Rehire
C	Pumpkin	_____	As well
D	Postponer's comment	_____	Beachwear
E	Erosion	_____	Idolater

THINK FAST QUIZ 9

This test measures your ability to follow directions under a strict time limit. You have exactly sixteen (16) minutes to read and answer the following questions. You need a pencil and the stopwatch to do this quiz. When the sixteen minutes are up, stop working, whether or not you're finished. Ready, set, go!

How many letters are in this sentence? _____. Leave this space blank _____ unless 3 + 3 = 7, in which case write SIX in the space. If MOTHER = 123456, what word is 34561215356? _____. In the diagram below, use eight of the nine words listed and create a crossword-style word square reading across and down. Also, circle the word in the word list that is not needed in the grid.

ALAS
ALOE
ASKS
COLA
CORK
KEYS
LACK
LAVA
VARY

		K	

What word can precede BOW, CHECK, DROP, and FOREST? _____. What is the answer when 3 x 9 x 27 is divided by 81? _____. If donkeys don't bray, write HEE-HAW in this blank: _____.

56

Divide the shape below along the lines to make two identical pieces with the same orientation.

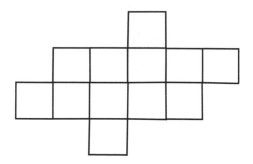

Put an X in this square ☐ if you think we've misspelled the word MISSPELLED in this sentence. Draw a wavy line under the largest of the following: the number of wheels on 8 tricycles and 3 bicycles; the total number of legs on 6 chickens and 4 dogs; lines in a sonnet plus golf course holes. Assume that no letters are left unread and only unread letters are considered useless. Can it be concluded that no letters are considered useless? Yes or no: _____. Pay no attention to the next sentence unless Stuttgart has four Ts. What word do you get if you remove four Ts from Stuttgart? _____. How much is a half-a-dozen dozen dimes worth? _____. In an alphabetical list, which of Snow White's dwarfs is last? _____. Add and subtract the letters in the names of the objects pictured below and write the final result here : _____.

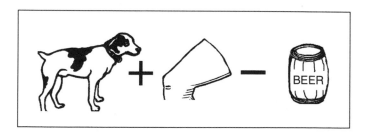

ANAGRAM QUIZ 3

Match each capitalized anagram with the definition of the anagram by writing the appropriate capital letter in the blank. For example, you would match the anagram ARCHES with the definition "Hunt," since ARCHES rearranges into SEARCH, which fits the definition. You have exactly twelve (12) minutes to read and match all four groups. If you finish early, give yourself an extra point for every full minute early that you finished. You need a pencil and the stopwatch to do this quiz. Ready, set, go!

Group One

A	Rubber source	_____	HAGS
B	Easily trained	_____	PANES
C	Deep cut	_____	COILED
D	Formal address	_____	OATEN
E	Make amends	_____	EXALT
F	Crescent moon, for one	_____	CHEEPS
G	Quaking tree	_____	HEAPS

Group Two

A	Sloppy brushstroke	_____	PIERCE
B	Cook's directions	_____	SEATS
C	Brunch, e.g.	_____	ICIEST
D	Valuable item	_____	LAME
E	Red gem	_____	CANOE
F	Map dots	_____	REAMS
G	Sea	_____	BURY

Group Three

A	Animal	_____	LACES
B	Plague of Egypt insect	_____	SHAM
C	Prepare potatoes	_____	MOCHA
D	Pastry chef	_____	ABETS
E	"You don't say!"	_____	BREAK
F	Butcher's device	_____	DENIED
G	Ridiculously manly	_____	CLOUTS

Group Four

A	Necklace fastener	_____	SIEVED
B	Prayer closing	_____	TABLE
C	Sort of tie	_____	SCALP
D	Think up	_____	CLEAN
E	Farm sound	_____	NAME
F	Jousting weapon	_____	DEEPLY
G	Expressed pain	_____	COAST

THINK FAST QUIZ 10

This test measures your ability to follow directions under a strict time limit. You have exactly fourteen (14) minutes to read and answer the following questions. You need a pencil and the stopwatch to do this quiz. When the fourteen minutes are up, stop working, whether or not you're finished. Ready, set, go!

Underline the word with the maximum number of letters in this particular sentence. What is the opposite of not true? _____. In the diagram below, make a word ladder than links BUY to FAD, changing only one letter at a time and always having a common word at each step.

BUY

___

___

FAD

Assume that ice cream is tasty and that no ice cream is ever eaten on Wednesdays. Can it be concluded that no tasty things are eaten on Wednesdays? Yes or no: _____. Ignore every third word in the following instruction: Draw a square triangle around inside this circle: O If LATE = 1234, what word is 3233143214 _____? Don't write FULL in this blank _____ unless empty is the opposite of full. List five 5-letter words that begin and end with E: _____ _____ _____ _____ _____. If today is Monday, what day of the week will it be 16 days from today? _____.

This pile of blocks is symmetric in all four directions. How many cubes were used to build it? _____.

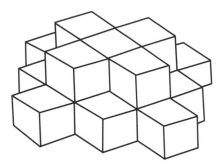

What word can precede ELEPHANT, FLAMINGO, LEMONADE, and SLIP? _____. Draw a wavy line under the fraction that is not equal to one-third: $^2/_6$, $^4/_{12}$, $^8/_{24}$, $^{17}/_{51}$, $^{32}/_{99}$, $^{123}/_{369}$. Read every second letter of these words and then write down what is being described: meow notch taffeta euro aspergill: _____. In the calendar below, cross out the last Saturday, the last Tuesday before the third Friday, and the second Monday after the last Saturday before the third Wednesday.

S	M	T	W	T	F	S
1	2	3	4	5	6	7
8	9	10	11	12	13	14
15	16	17	18	19	20	21
22	23	24	25	26	27	28
29	30					

Don't forget to neglect writing DNE in reverse order here: _____.

50/50 TRIVIA QUIZ 10

 For each statement circle the correct word from the two below it. You have exactly three (3) minutes to read and answer the following questions. When the three minutes are up, stop working. Ready, set, go!

1. Length of the original "Star Trek" mission

   5 years   10 years

2. Auckland's country

   Australia   New Zealand

3. Farsightedness

   hyperopia   myopia

4. Number of lanes in an Olympic swimming pool

   6   8

5. Largest terrier

   Airedale   Aberdeen

6. Winston Churchill's Nobel Prize category

   Literature   Peace

7. Skunk in the film *Bambi*

   Flower   Petunia

8. Fencing term for jump + lunge

   balestra   fleche

9. The "O" in OPEC

   oil   organization

10. Where loofah sponges grow
    land   ocean

11. Elizabeth II's coronation year
    1952   1957

12. Cathedral bordering Moscow's Red Square
    St. Basil's   St. Peter's

13. Mother of Horus, in Egyptian myth
    Isis   Nut

14. Most likely sum when you toss two dice
    6   7

15. Master gland of the endrocrine system
    pituitary   thyroid

16. Rival gang of the Jets in *West Side Story*
    Sharks   Tigers

17. Composer of the *Goldberg Variations*
    Bach   Vivaldi

18. President who wrote *Profiles in Courage*
    FDR   JFK

19. Most abundant element in our solar system
    hydrogen   helium

20. Sabena Airlines home country
    Belgium   Brazil

SCRAMBLE UP QUIZ 3

Insert a letter into each capitalized word and then rearrange these letters to form a new word, and match the result with a definition on the right. Write the added letter in the blank beside the definition. For example, given ONION, you can insert T and rearrange to make NOTION and then write the letter T in the blank beside the definition "Thought." As a bonus, the filled blanks in each grouping spell a common English word. You have exactly fifteen (15) minutes to match all five groups. If you finish early, give yourself an extra point for every full minute early that you finished. You need a pencil and the stopwatch to do this quiz. Ready, set, go!

Group One

AGENT	_____	Close at hand
CEASE	_____	Reptile with a shell
OVINE	_____	Having a meal
UTTER	_____	Rap session?
YEARN	_____	Call upon

Group Two

CURSE	_____	Building with minarets
MOUSE	_____	Sheriff's aide
PEACE	_____	China cup carrier
SLICE	_____	Get free
TYPED	_____	Sculptor's tool

Group Three

IMAGE	_____	Quick look
ANGEL	_____	Sunday delivery
OMENS	_____	Proverb
FIELD	_____	Trinket-stealing bird
GAINS	_____	Used a crane

Group Four

THIGH	_____	Spicy sausage
DINGO	_____	Prayer beads
SORRY	_____	Arsenic or cyanide
SNOOP	_____	Catching 40 winks
ALIAS	_____	Mount Everest's is 8848 m

Group Five

CHOIR	_____	Born first
CRANE	_____	Brave
INFER	_____	Place for bats?
STEEL	_____	Eye's "window"
BERYL	_____	Persian carpet's decorative border

THINK FAST QUIZ 11

This test measures your ability to follow directions under a strict time limit. You have exactly sixteen (16) minutes to read and answer the following questions. You need a pencil and the stopwatch to do this quiz. When the sixteen minutes are up, stop working, whether or not you're finished. Ready, set, go!

Circle the only word in this sentence with the same number of letters as the word immediately following it. Write SATURN in this blank _____ unless Venus and Mars are planets. If the initial letters of "like it or not" spell the name of an animal, write the final letters of "live in a dream" in reverse order in this space: _____. In the diagram below, use the nine letters of the word SATELLITE, one letter per square, to complete a word square with four words reading across and four others reading down.

Multiply 4 times 13 times 25: _____. If Amsterdam is the city where most American football is played, write DUTCH TOWN in this blank: _____.

Otherwise, write the word you get when you spoonerize the phrase DUTCH TOWN.

	T		W
		V	A
	X	I	
W			

Divide the shape below along the lines to make two identical pieces with the same orientation.

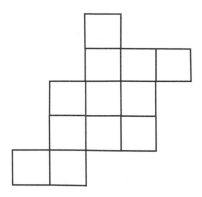

List three common 4-letter words that begin with UN: _____ _____ _____. On a test, Greg scored higher than Fred, but Ethel scored higher than Greg. Fred outscored Dora, and Harry scored lower than Greg. Must Harry have outscored Dora? ____. Must Greg have outscored Fred by more than he outscored Dora? _____. In the card layout below, circle three cards of the same suit that total 15. Circle the word that doesn't come from French: boudoir, pretzel, denim, pansy. Assume that some people like apples and that some people are teachers. Can it be concluded that some teachers like apples? Yes or no: _____. Write the number of half-dozens in a gross here _____ unless there are 12 items in a half-dozen. If you see the word underline anywhere on this page, underline it. If rowing is not a sport, insert an R into the center of the word LEANED and write the result here: _____. Otherwise, write only the letters in the even-numbered positions of the word LEANED in the space.

LETTER INSERTION QUIZ 2

Insert a letter into each capitalized word to form a new word, and match the result with a definition on the right. Write the added letter in the blank beside the definition. For example, given CURSE, you can insert O to make COURSE and then write the letter O in the blank beside the definition "school offering." As a bonus, the filled blanks in each grouping spell a common English word. You have exactly ten (10) minutes to match all five groups. If you finish early, give yourself an extra point for every full minute early that you finished. You need a pencil and the stopwatch to do this quiz. Ready, set, go!

Group One

FLEES	_____	Marked by turbulent weather
HERON	_____	Source of addiction
STORY	_____	Shows off at the gym

Group Two

BACON	_____	Horse's home
SEWER	_____	For the most part
MANLY	_____	Shish-kebab stick
STALE	_____	Guiding light

Group Three

BERET	_____	Not as tangy
FIGHT	_____	Prepared beer or tea
MILER	_____	Smart
BREED	_____	Horror flick reaction
BRINY	_____	Deprived (of)

Group Four

BUSES	_____	Pro
METER	_____	Swivel, as hips
GRATE	_____	Born here
PRICE	_____	Thick tails
NAIVE	_____	Shooting star
EXERT	_____	Queen's boy

Group Five

CAUSE	_____	Quit in chess
TREAD	_____	Hindu wonder-workers: Var.
FAIRS	_____	One in a lineup
INSET	_____	Devise
QUEER	_____	Contract provision
REIGN	_____	Bug
CRATE	_____	Bobbin stuff

THINK FAST QUIZ 12

 This test measures your ability to follow directions under a strict time limit. You have exactly fifteen (15) minutes to read and answer the following questions. You need a pencil and the stopwatch to do this quiz. When the fifteen minutes are up, stop working, whether or not you're finished. Ready, set, go!

Draw a line under the third D in this sentence. What 7-letter word appears backward in 7 consecutive letters in the word FLAGELLIFORM? _____. Assume that anyone who tries hard is not a nincompoop and that all happy people try hard. Can it be concluded that no happy people are nincompoops? Yes or no: _____. This pile of blocks in the diagram at the right is symmetric in all four directions. How many cubes were used to build it? _____. If oxygen isn't a chemical element, write LEAD here _____, unless lead is a chemical element, in which case don't write anything. I have some cupcakes. When I give away half of my cupcakes plus half a cupcake, I have 15 cupcakes left. How many cupcakes did I originally have? _____. Think of two 5-letter words that have a Y in the third position and no other vowels: _____ _____. If ferns are musical instruments, write NO here: _____. Otherwise, shift each letter of FERNS back four places in the alphabet and write the result instead.

Which number between 25 and 45 doesn't appear in the
diagram below? _____.

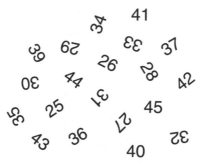

Think of a digit. Add 4. Multiply by your digit. Add 4. Take the
square root, and then subtract your digit. Write the result here:
_____. In the diagram below, how many ways are there to travel
along the lines from P to Q if
you may go up and right
only? _____. Circle the
word in which every letter
appears exactly twice:
appeases, rendered,
commence, iffiness. In an

alphabetical list, which of the 12 zodiac signs is first?
_____. Pay no attention to the next sentence unless water
isn't wet. Write water's chemical formula: _____. If DUN is
not a color, write BROWN in this blank: _____.
Otherwise, write a four-letter homophone of DUN.

SCRAMBLE UP QUIZ 4

Insert a letter into each capitalized word and then rearrange these letters to form a new word, and match the result with a definition on the right. Write the added letter in the blank beside the definition. For example, given ONION, you can insert T and rearrange to make NOTION and then write the letter T in the blank beside the definition "Thought." As a bonus, the filled blanks in each grouping spell a common English word. You have exactly twelve (12) minutes to match all five groups. If you finish early, give yourself an extra point for every full minute early that you finished. You need a pencil and the stopwatch to do this quiz. Ready, set, go!

Group One

ACORN	_____	Ancient Egyptian writer
AGAIN	_____	Turn on an axis
CRAFT	_____	Coloring book colorer
CRIES	_____	3 or 5, to 15
OTTER	_____	Arboreal lizard

Group Two

DRIES	_____	Prime time TV offering
EASES	_____	Magazine supplement
MOIST	_____	Clothing
STEIN	_____	Hamburger bun seed
TREAT	_____	Tarantula, e.g.

Group Three

CELLO	_____	Tell
CIGAR	_____	Vampire-repelling bulb
MINOR	_____	Story setting
STORE	_____	Union action
TRIES	_____	Seafood needing shucking

Group Four

APRON	_____	Known to all
FOAMS	_____	Mystery
IMAGE	_____	Pitched, as a baseball
NORTH	_____	In recent days
TALLY	_____	Release from death row

Group Five

ALIEN	_____	Cower
CANOE	_____	Take a breath
NICER	_____	Newspaper bigwig
THIEF	_____	Fixation
TRIED	_____	Gas pump number

THINK FAST QUIZ 13

 This test measures your ability to follow directions under a strict time limit. You have exactly sixteen (16) minutes to read and answer the following questions. You need a pencil and the stopwatch to do this quiz. When the sixteen minutes are up, stop working, whether or not you're finished. Ready, set, go!

Among the letters A to M of the alphabet, which is the only one that doesn't appear in this sentence? _____. If squeezing an orange doesn't give milk, write JUICE here: _____. If tomorrow is Tuesday, what day of the week will it be five days after the day before yesterday? _____. How many triangles (of any size) are in diagram at the right? _____. If we don't get milk from cows, draw a circle in this square ☐ , but if we do, leave it blank and answer the negative of the following question incorrectly: what year is it? _____. Divide 100 by ½ and add 50: _____.

Count the number of hyphens in the next sentence and write the answer here: _____. My know-it-all, ne'er-do-well mother-in-law did a man-in-the-street interview with an aide-de-camp holding a hand-me-down jack-in-the-box.

In the calendar below, draw a square around any 3 x 3 set of calendar numbers. Add up all nine numbers in the squares you drew, divide the result by the middle number, and write your answer here: _____.

S	M	T	W	T	F	S
1	2	3	4	5	6	7
8	9	10	11	12	13	14
15	16	17	18	19	20	21
22	23	24	25	26	27	28
29	30	31				

If there are 20 matches in a standard pack of matches, write half of that amount here: _____. Otherwise, write double the amount instead. In the diagram below, make a word ladder that links OIL to RIG, changing only one letter at a time and always having a common word at each step.

OIL

___

___

___

RIG

Assume that if it has rained then the grass is wet, and that it hasn't rained. Must the grass be dry? _____. Circle the word that doesn't become a new word when the M is turned upside-down to become a W: MISER, CLAMS, SMEAR, MATCH, COMER, SCRAM. Three children share 30 cookies. Pam eats 6 times as many as Sam, and Cam eats 6 more than Sam. How many did Sam eat? _____. List three countries that end with the letter L: _____ _____ _____. Read each word of this sentence in reverse order and answer in the space provided: tahW seod "STOP" lleps drawkcab? _____.

BRAIN STRETCHERS QUIZ 4

Match each item on the left with one on the right by writing the appropriate capital letter in the blank. The matches are based on similar meanings, but watch out for tricky wordplay including double meanings and altered spacing within words. For example, you would match "anti-diplomacy" with "contact" (con tact). You have exactly twelve (12) minutes to read and match all five groups. If you finish early, give yourself an extra point for every full minute early that you finished. You need a pencil and the stopwatch to do this quiz. Ready, set, go!

Group One

A Everest   _____ Housecoat
B Cold shower   _____ Office
C Paint   _____ Hail
D Camping   _____ Amount
E Serving a hockey penalty   _____ Intent

Group Two

A Frame of mind   _____ Junk mail
B Monarchistic   _____ Skull
C Noticed   _____ Peruvian lineage
D Frequent flyers   _____ Forking
E Incandescent   _____ Without frosting

Group Three

A	Eye makeup	_____	My fish
B	Igloo	_____	Big bench
C	Scorer's job	_____	Cornea, iris, pupil, etc.
D	Subsample	_____	Totally
E	Bassinet	_____	Northern hemisphere

Group Four

A	Copper band	_____	Ocean liner
B	Sand	_____	Kiss and make up
C	Endanger	_____	Paper clip
D	Office holder	_____	Hebrides
E	Grooms	_____	Posse

Group Five

A	Superconductor	_____	Toasty
B	Thimble	_____	Maestro
C	Beaten	_____	Sewer cover
D	Pig's destination	_____	Wearing ring
E	Abandon	_____	Rate highly

ANSWERS

50/50 Trivia Quiz 1
1. white
2. omega
3. 1600
4. hair
5. bauxite
6. bishop
7. 2
8. Austen
9. Post
10. *vendredi*

Anagram Quiz 1
Score one point for each answer in the correct blank. Add one point for every full minute early that you finished.

Group One
G INBRED
D LAMP
B EDIBLE
F CHINA
A RABID
C BAGEL
E ATTIC

Group Two
F BUSTED
A ZEBRA
E SCARE
B BISTRO
D EASY
G WASTE
C MARCH

Group Three
E DREAD
C CIRCLE
F CEDAR
G THAW
B SAUCE
D DECREE
A BRIBED

Group Four
B CROCUS
F ARGON
G EASEL
A SOFA
C DANCE
E BOWL
D EXTRA

Ratings:
28+: You have an amazing ability to anagram quickly.
24-27: Excellent! Your letter rearrangement abilities are outstanding
20-23: Very good! You worked very well under pressure.
16-19: Good. You did some good solid anagramming.
Less than 15: You needed to scramble a bit more for some answers!

Think Fast Quiz 1
1. Eight
2. 62
3. No. (If it's a fish, it's not winged, and we have no information about non-winged creatures.)
4. 16
5. SWIMS (Looks the same either way up.)
6. Star
7. This space should be blank.
8. Five (Barb gets 15)
9. TOASTER (Starting at the lower left, spiral inward to spell the message "Kitchen appliance that cooks bread.")
10. The letter T should be in the next space.
11. Circle ABILY (Libya). All the rest are anagrams of animals (camel, zebra, tiger).
12. Any 5 of: batik, black, blank, bleak, blink, block, break, brick, brink, brisk, brook.
13. TRUE
14. The circle containing the number 1 should be circled.
15. END

79

Score one point for each complete and correct answer. The maximum score is 15.
Ratings:
15: Amazing! You have an outstanding ability to think clearly under pressure.
13-14: Excellent! You kept focused throughout a tough challenge.
10-12: Very good! You probably keep on top of things both at work and at home.
7-9: OK. You solved several puzzles, but may have tripped up on others because of time pressures.
4-6: Fair. Some of this quiz's instructions were too tricky for you.
0-3: This type of timed test may not be your strong suit.

50/50 Trivia Quiz 2

1. Switzerland
2. entomology
3. Pisces
4. Bronze
5. Alabama
6. Austria
7. Chaney
8. femur
9. 20
10. Tehran
11. 7 months
12. Sicily
13. 1950s
14. Germany
15. Dostoyevsky
16. Oscar
17. da Vinci
18. *glasnost*
19. 5
20. day

Score one point for each complete and correct answer. The maximum score is 20.
Ratings:
20: Outstanding! You're a trivia whiz!
18-19: Excellent! You know a lot of useless stuff.
15-17: Very good! You are able to choose well under pressure.
11-14: Good. You may have found that you needed to guess on a few...hope some of them worked in your favor.
10: Hmmm...You should expect the same score if you guessed at random.
0-9: Selecting at random might have worked better for you!

Letter Insertion Quiz 1

Score one point for each correct letter. Add one point for every full minute early that you finished.

Group One
P STA(P)LE
E SUR(E)LY
W SHRE(W)D

Group Two
B RO(B)UST
I D(I)ETER
L CAST(L)E
L PART(L)Y

Group Three
F STI(F)LE
R C(R)ATER
O GR(O)OVE
C PLA(C)ID
K MON(K)EY

Group Four
J IN(J)URE
O L(O)ATHE
S CO(S)MIC
H RIC(H)ER
E S(E)WING
D DE(D)UCE

Group Five
A P(A)LACE
U D(U)RESS
G BRID(G)E
M RE(M)EDY
E D(E)RIVE
N FRIE(N)D
T GUES(T)S

Ratings:
25+: Wow! This is an amazing letter-insertion score!
21-24: Excellent! You were almost letter-perfect!
17-20: Very good! Most of the letters fell into place.
Less than 17: You slipped a bit in slipping in letters.

Think Fast Quiz 2

1. G
2. V W X Y Z
3. BIRD
4. 9
5. wayward
6. 10
7. Any 5 of Iceland, India, Indonesia, Iran, Iraq, Ireland, Israel, Italy, Ivory Coast.
8. The bottom middle toothpick should be crossed out, like this:

9. SINGALONG
10. Underline "equation"
11. This space should be empty.
12. 12 (Peg has 6 and Reg has 3)
13. S U B
    P R O
    A N Y
14. No. (Perhaps all people wear both, crass or polite.)
15. DONE

Score one point for each complete and correct answer. The maximum score is 15.
Ratings:
15: Amazing! You have an outstanding ability to think clearly under pressure.
13-14: Excellent! You kept focused throughout a tough challenge.
10-12: Very good! You probably keep on top of things both at work and at home.
7-9: OK. You solved several puzzles, but may have tripped up on others because of time pressures.
4-6: Fair. Some of this quiz's instructions were too tricky for you.
0-3: This type of timed test may not be your strong suit.

Brain Stretchers Quiz 1

Score one point for each answer in the correct blank. Add one point for every full minute early that you finished.

Group One
B   down = feathers
C
E
A   Butt-er
D   8 ball in billiards

Group Two
D
E
B   Train-ee
C   Co-aches
A   Go at

Group Three
C   Ex-press
D   Dent-ists
A
E
B   A drove of cattle

Group Four
E
A
D   Ram parts
B
C   Moo ragcs

Group Five
B   De-pressing
E   Parch-ment
D
C   Trip-lets
A   Do grace

Ratings:
25+: Wow! Your brain is quite nimble.
21-24: Excellent! Your ability to spot relationships is well developed.
17-20: Very good! Your brain is alive and kicking.
13-16: Good. You thought your way through several pairings.
Less than 13: Your brain may need a kick-start!

Think Fast Quiz 3

1. START
2. The capital C after the word "letter" should be circled.
3. The first blank should contain LIMES. The next blank should be empty.
4.
5. Easy
6. RUBBER
7. This space should be blank.
8. LEFT
9. ⊕
10. No. (Perhaps I enjoy anything amusing and anything not amusing.)
11. Circle basset. (The others sound like: thimble, growth, faithful, unthinkable.)
12. 24
13. hamster, hedgehog, hippopotamus, horse, hyena, etc.
14.

7	8	3	9	2	8	1	3
6	5	2	8	5	6	7	2
3	1	4	7	1	4	5	6
5	2	9	6	2	9	3	1
7	8	1	5	3	7	4	2
9	4	3	7	8	1	5	8
1	2	5	1	2	9	4	6
4	6	7	4	6	3	2	1

15. FINISH (in, fish)

Score one point for each complete and correct answer. The maximum score is 15.
Ratings:
15: Amazing! You have an outstanding ability to think clearly under pressure.
13-14: Excellent! You kept focused throughout a tough challenge.
10-12: Very good! You probably keep on top of things both at work and at home.
7-9: OK. You solved several puzzles, but may have tripped up on others because of time pressures.
4-6: Fair. Some of this quiz's instructions were too tricky for you.
0-3: This type of timed test may not be your strong suit.

50/50 Trivia Quiz 3

1. T
2. amber
3. Amsterdam
4. penicillin
5. Miller
6. Islamabad
7. scallops
8. Fitzgerald
9. skulk
10. July 14
11. Minnesota
12. Second
13. Mars
14. Incan
15. Van Gogh
16. obtuse
17. maxilla
18. Perseus
19. Loire
20. barrels

Score one point for each complete and correct answer. The maximum score is 20.
Ratings:
20: Outstanding! You're a trivia whiz!
18-19: Excellent! You know a lot of useless stuff.
15-17: Very good! You are able to choose well under pressure.
11-14: Good. You may have found that you needed to guess on a few...hope some of them worked in your favor.
10: Hmmm...You should expect the same score if you guessed at random.
0-9: Selecting at random might have worked better for you!

50/50 Trivia Quiz 4

1. Macedonia
2. heart
3. Libya
4. Saturn
5. War of 1812
6. October
7. kitten
8. Rembrandt
9. cone
10. steel
11. Best
12. Kelly
13. 1789
14. chromium
15. teeth
16. Saudi Arabia
17. 12
18. Wells
19. Italian
20. 28 years

Score one point for each complete and correct answer.
The maximum score is 20.
Ratings:
20: Outstanding! You're a trivia whiz!
18-19: Excellent! You know a lot of useless stuff.
15-17: Very good! You are able to choose well under
pressure.
11-14: Good. You may have found that you needed to
guess on a few...hope some of them worked in your
favor.
10: Hmmm...You should expect the same score if you
guessed at random.
0-9: Selecting at random might have worked better for
you!

Scramble Up Quiz 1

Score one point for each correct letter.
Add one point for every full minute
early that you finished.

Group One
C   giant; acting
U   taste; statue
R   demon; modern
V   bread; adverb
Y   mauls; asylum

Group Two
F   triad; adrift
I   dream; admire
G   early; argyle
H   edict; itched
T   later; rattle

Group Three
E   latch; chalet
L   nomad; almond
B   lutes; subtle
O   pride; period
W   amiss; swamis

Group Four
S   rupee; peruse
P   arose; operas
A   pride; diaper
N   chest; stench
K   curse; sucker

Group Five
M   leads; damsel
I   spear; praise
X   douse; exodus
E   tarry; artery
D   yeast; steady

Ratings:
25+: Wow! You added a little something extra to your
solving!
21-24: Excellent! Practically flawless in the mix.
17-20: Very good! You found many of the anagrams.
Less than 17: Well, you were scrambling.

Think Fast Quiz 4

1. The second N of the word "counting" should be crossed off.
2. The capital F at the end of the sentence should be crossed off.
3. POTS & PANS
4. The first blank should be empty, and the second blank should contain TWO.
5. 10 rectangles
6. Underline "expandable." (The hidden birds are: raven, robin, crow, wren.)
7. The next line should have three Xs above it.
8. Yes
9. 7H, KD, 3S
10. 16
11. Put a box around "prowl."
12. Any two of: silicon, silver, sulfur
13. Number 8
14. S
15. QUIT

Score one point for each complete and correct answer. The maximum score is 15.

Ratings:

15: Amazing! You have an outstanding ability to think clearly under pressure.

13-14: Excellent! You kept focused throughout a tough challenge.

10-12: Very good! You probably keep on top of things both at work and at home.

7-9: OK. You solved several puzzles, but may have tripped up on others because of time pressures.

4-6: Fair. Some of this quiz's instructions were too tricky for you.

0-3: This type of timed test may not be your strong suit.

Anagram Quiz 2

Score one point for each answer in the correct blank. Add one point for every full minute early that you finished.

Group One

G GASES
E TRAY
A AGREE
C LARGE
F GIANTS
B SAFER
D SIGNAL

Group Two

C ANGEL
G ADORE
D NATION
B PASS
A FALSE
E GRAPE
F ARTIST

Group Three

D PARSON
F RUNWAY
B TAIL
E MANGO
C ANGST
G MANY
A LEASH

Group Four

F SALT
A DEBRIS
E FLOAT
G ASKEW
D SUBTLE
C HEART
B ANGER

Ratings:

28+: You have an amazing ability to anagram quickly.

24-27: Excellent! Your letter rearrangement abilities are outstanding.

20-23: Very good! You worked very well under pressure.

16-19: Good. You did some good solid anagramming.

Less than 15: You needed to scramble a bit more for some answers!

Think Fast Quiz 5

1. The *a* in "unusual" and the *e* in "under" should be circled.
2. The blank should be empty.
3. 50 cubes
4. SENSELESSNESS
5. Monday
6. Dip, tip, tap, tar, oar (other answers are possible)
7. Six (How many legs do ants have?)
8. Yes (All jugglers are clowns, who are not funny. So no funny people juggle.)
9. Ice
10. The next space should contain the word MAIL.
11. Underline "amongst"
12. peep, plop, pomp, pulp, pump, etc.
13. $16
14. The word "hands" should be circled.
15. FINALE

Score one point for each complete and correct answer. The maximum score is 15.
Ratings:
15: Amazing! You have an outstanding ability to think clearly under pressure.
13-14: Excellent! You kept focused throughout a tough challenge.
10-12: Very good! You probably keep on top of things both at work and at home.
7-9: OK. You solved several puzzles, but may have tripped up on others because of time pressures.
4-6: Fair. Some of this quiz's instructions were too tricky for you.
0-3: This type of timed test may not be your strong suit.

50/50 Trivia Quiz 5

1. silver
2. i.e.
3. Haile Selassie
4. Quebec
5. Confucius
6. wallaby
7. Botticelli
8. XIX
9. June
10. Siam
11. Doc
12. My Struggle
13. Iago
14. XX
15. lighthouse
16. Schubert
17. Florence
18. Venus
19. eggs
20. Bunyan

Score one point for each complete and correct answer. The maximum score is 20.
Ratings:
20: Outstanding! You're a trivia whiz!
18-19: Excellent! You know a lot of useless stuff.
15-17: Very good! You are able to choose well under pressure.
11-14: Good. You may have found that you needed to guess on a few...hope some of them worked in your favor.
10: Hmmm...You should expect the same score if you guessed at random.
0-9: Selecting at random might have worked better for you!

50/50 Trivia Quiz 6

1. enroll
2. Nero
3. Bradbury
4. 206
5. barber
6. Liechtenstein
7. Korean
8. Tchaikovsky
9. Flagg
10. mercury
11. Deuteronomy
12. Cu
13. human
14. 2
15. Feb 2
16. Versailles
17. 90°
18. Jupiter
19. 10
20. postcards

Score one point for each complete and correct answer.
The maximum score is 20.
Ratings:
20: Outstanding! You're a trivia whiz!
18-19: Excellent! You know a lot of useless stuff.
15-17: Very good! You are able to choose well under pressure.
11-14: Good. You may have found that you needed to guess on a few...hope some of them worked in your favor.
10: Hmmm...You should expect the same score if you guessed at random.
0-9: Selecting at random might have worked better for you!

Think Fast Quiz 6

1. BEGIN
2. Nine
3.
4. Four
5. HOT
6. 34 (thirty plus four)
7. Mexico, Monaco, Morocco
8. No. (There is no guarantee that the two groups studying economics have an overlap.)
9. Pipe
10. The calendar numbers 7, 24, and 25 should be crossed off.
11. THEREAFTER
12. Seven
13. The next space should contain the word LEVEL. (Carpenters often own planes for planing wood.)
14. The next space should contain the word BALLOON.
15. STOP

Score one point for each complete and correct answer.
The maximum score is 15.
Ratings:
15: Amazing! You have an outstanding ability to think clearly under pressure.
13-14: Excellent! You kept focused throughout a tough challenge.
10-12: Very good! You probably keep on top of things both at work and at home.
7-9: OK. You solved several puzzles, but may have tripped up on others because of time pressures.
4-6: Fair. Some of this quiz's instructions were too tricky for you.
0-3: This type of timed test may not be your strong suit.

50/50 Trivia Quiz 7

1. Fe
2. Pasteur
3. slowly
4. Irish Sea
5. St. Jude
6. skin
7. Degas
8. ohm
9. Dallas
10. Switzerland
11. *mariposa*
12. zero
13. Hilton
14. Venus
15. Africa
16. 7
17. cheetah
18. Chopin
19. scapula
20. Dutch

Score one point for each complete and correct answer. The maximum score is 20.
Ratings:
20: Outstanding! You're a trivia whiz!
18-19: Excellent! You know a lot of useless stuff.
15-17: Very good! You are able to choose well under pressure.
11-14: Good. You may have found that you needed to guess on a few...hope some of them worked in your favor.
10: Hmmm...You should expect the same score if you guessed at random.
0-9: Selecting at random might have worked better for you!

Brain Stretchers Quiz 2

Score one point for each answer in the correct blank. Add one point for every full minute early that you finished.

Group One
C   Pre-late
E
A
B   Bi-shop
D

Group Two
D   Re-treat
A
E
C   Sin king
B   For tresses

Group Three
E   Imp action
D   Grate-ful
B   Anti-body
A   (William) Tell tale target
C   Drum sticks

Group Four
B
C   Plan gent
D   In stance
E   Book of Job
A

Group Five
C
A   Ra is in
E   De-liberate
B   Ass-ess
D

Ratings:
25+: Wow! Your brain is quite nimble.
21-24: Excellent! Your ability to spot relationships is well developed.
17-20: Very good! Your brain is alive and kicking.
13-16: Good. You thought your way through several pairings.
Less than 13: Your brain may need a kick-start!

Think Fast Quiz 7

1. 21
2. Midas
3. FOOT
4. 7:23
5. The next blank should be empty.
6. Thirty (9 + 2 + 8 + 1 + 10)
7. No. (Possibly all terriers are happy, too.)
8. Elephant. (Rearrange the eight chunks to spell the message "ani/mal/ wit/h tu/sks/ and/ a/ trunk.")
9. word
10. 32
11. 5 times
12. 27
13. September
14. This space should be blank.
15. COMPLETE

Score one point for each complete and correct answer.
The maximum score is 15.
Ratings:
15: Amazing! You have an outstanding ability to think clearly under pressure.
13-14: Excellent! You kept focused throughout a tough challenge.
10-12: Very good! You probably keep on top of things both at work and at home.
7-9: OK. You solved several puzzles, but may have tripped up on others because of time pressures.
4-6: Fair. Some of this quiz's instructions were too tricky for you.
0-3: This type of timed test may not be your strong suit.

Scramble Up Quiz 2

Score one point for each correct letter.
Add one point for every full minute early that you finished.

Group One

M bluer; lumber
A three; heater
J nosey; enjoys
O eight; hogtie
R squat; quarts

Group Two

F onset; soften
L mason; salmon
I start; artist
C score; soccer
K opens; spoken

Group Three

B short; throbs
U tango; nougat
S suite; tissue
H since; inches
Y grind; drying

Group Four

G ebony; bygone
I asset; siesta
V skein; knives
E warns; answer
N tease; senate

Group Five

D hairs; radish
W early; lawyer
E mirth; hermit
L ratio; tailor
T panic; catnip

Ratings:
25+: Wow! You added a little something extra to your solving!
21-24: Excellent! Practically flawless in the mix.
17-20: Very good! You found many of the anagrams.
Less than 17: Well, you were scrambling.

Think Fast Quiz 8

1. Nineteen
2. PRECIPICE
3. Right
4. W
5. 13 equilateral triangles
6. napkin, neaten, notion, etc.
7. The first blank should say YES and the second blank should say NO.
8. The 10 and 4 of clubs in the top row should be circled.
9. Cool and nervous should be underlined.
10.

6	8	11	5
13	3	0	14
1	15	12	2
10	4	7	9

11. House
12. YES should be written at the top of the page.
13. 175
14. Wednesday
15. END

Score one point for each complete and correct answer. The maximum score is 15.
Ratings:
15: Amazing! You have an outstanding ability to think clearly under pressure.
13-14: Excellent! You kept focused throughout a tough challenge.
10-12: Very good! You probably keep on top of things both at work and at home.
7-9: OK. You solved several puzzles, but may have tripped up on others because of time pressures.
4-6: Fair. Some of this quiz's instructions were too tricky for you.
0-3: This type of timed test may not be your strong suit.

50/50 Trivia Quiz 8

1. Latin
2. Earth
3. corn
4. Sb
5. Rolls-Royce
6. hippopotamus
7. Nepal
8. More
9. Key Largo
10. Dali
11. pollex
12. Goodyear
13. Diana
14. Keynes
15. 3600
16. whalebone
17. *Hamlet*
18. Rome
19. Ruff
20. Italy

Score one point for each complete and correct answer. The maximum score is 20.
Ratings:
20: Outstanding! You're a trivia whiz!
18-19: Excellent! You know a lot of useless stuff.
15-17: Very good! You are able to choose well under pressure.
11-14: Good. You may have found that you needed to guess on a few...hope some of them worked in your favor.
10: Hmmm...You should expect the same score if you guessed at random.
0-9: Selecting at random might have worked better for you!

50/50 Trivia Quiz 9

1. libel
2. H_2SO_4
3. flags
4. Istanbul
5. leather
6. 32
7. Harvard
8. Babe
9. Korean
10. tin
11. 2
12. green
13. Emily
14. duck
15. Kublai
16. 3rd
17. Jupiter
18. Loki
19. 24
20. Gauguin

Score one point for each complete and correct answer. The maximum score is 20.
Ratings:
20: Outstanding! You're a trivia whiz!
18-19: Excellent! You know a lot of useless stuff.
15-17: Very good! You are able to choose well under pressure.
11-14: Good. You may have found that you needed to guess on a few...hope some of them worked in your favor.
10: Hmmm...You should expect the same score if you guessed at random.
0-9: Selecting at random might have worked better for you!

Brain Stretchers Quiz 3

Score one point for each answer in the correct blank. Add one point for every full minute early that you finished.

Group One

D
A   Cap on
E
C   Non-plus
B   St. Arches

Group Two

C
D
B   Maltese cross
E   Wand-er
A

Group Three

B
C   Web-ster
D
A   Co-wed
E

Group Four

E
A
D
B
C   In firm

Group Five

C   Pump kin
A   De-terminate
B   A swell
E   Beach wear
D   I do later

Ratings:
25+: Wow! Your brain is quite nimble.
21-24: Excellent! Your ability to spot relationships is well-developed.
17-20: Very good! Your brain is alive and kicking.
13-16: Good. You thought your way through several pairings.
Less than 13: Your brain may need a kick-start!

Think Fast Quiz 9

1. Thirty-one
2. This space should be blank.
3. THERMOMETER
4. The word COLA in the word list should be circled.

    L A C K
    A L O E
    V A R Y
    A S K S
5. Rain
6. Nine
7. This blank should be empty.
8.

9. The square should not have an X in it.
10. A wavy line should be drawn under "lines in a sonnet plus golf course holes" (14 + 18 = 32); the other answers are 30 and 28, respectively
11. Yes
12. Sugar
13. $7.20
14. Sneezy
15. DONE (dog + knee − keg)

Score one point for each complete and correct answer. The maximum score is 15.

Ratings:

15: Amazing! You have an outstanding ability to think clearly under pressure.

13-14: Excellent! You kept focused throughout a tough challenge.

10-12: Very good! You probably keep on top of things both at work and at home.

7-9: OK. You solved several puzzles, but may have tripped up on others because of time pressures.

4-6: Fair. Some of this quiz's instructions were too tricky for you.

0-3: This type of timed test may not be your strong suit.

Anagram Quiz 3

Score one point for each answer in the correct blank. Add one point for every full minute early that you finished.

Group One

C GASH
G ASPEN
B DOCILE
E ATONE
A LATEX
D SPEECH
F PHASE

Group Two

B RECIPE
D ASSET
F CITIES
C MEAL
G OCEAN
A SMEAR
E RUBY

Group Three

F SCALE
C MASH
G MACHO
A BEAST
D BAKER
E INDEED
B LOCUST

Group Four

D DEVISE
E BLEAT
A CLASP
F LANCE
B AMEN
G YELPED
C ASCOT

Ratings:

28+: You have an amazing ability to anagram quickly.

24-27: Excellent! Your letter rearrangement abilities are outstanding

20-23: Very good! You worked very well under pressure.

16-19: Good. You did some good solid anagramming.

Less than 15: You needed to scramble a bit more for some answers!

Think Fast Quiz 10

1. The word "particular" should be underlined.
2. True
3. Buy, bud, bad, fad.
4. No
5. The circle should have a triangle drawn around it.
6. TATTLETALE
7. FULL
8. Eagle, eerie, elite, elope, erase, etc.
9. Wednesday
10. 18 cubes
11. Pink
12. Draw a wavy line under $^{32}/_{99}$.
13. May (month after April)
14. The calendar numbers 28, 17, and 23 should be crossed out.
15. END

Score one point for each complete and correct answer. The maximum score is 15.
Ratings:
15: Amazing! You have an outstanding ability to think clearly under pressure.
13-14: Excellent! You kept focused throughout a tough challenge.
10-12: Very good! You probably keep on top of things both at work and at home.
7-9: OK. You solved several puzzles, but may have tripped up on others because of time pressures.
4-6: Fair. Some of this quiz's instructions were too tricky for you.
0-3: This type of timed test may not be your strong suit.

50/50 Trivia Quiz 10

1. 5 years
2. New Zealand
3. hyperopia
4. 8
5. Airedale
6. Literature
7. Flower
8. balestra
9. organization
10. land
11. 1952
12. St. Basil's
13. Isis
14. 7
15. pituitary
16. Sharks
17. Bach
18. JFK
19. hydrogen
20. Belgium

Score one point for each complete and correct answer. The maximum score is 20.
Ratings:
20: Outstanding! You're a trivia whiz!
18-19: Excellent! You know a lot of useless stuff.
15-17: Very good! You are able to choose well under pressure.
11-14: Good. You may have found that you needed to guess on a few...hope some of them worked in your favor.
10: Hmmm...You should expect the same score if you guessed at random.
0-9: Selecting at random might have worked better for you!

Scramble Up Quiz 3

Score one point for each correct letter.
Add one point for every full minute early that you finished.

Group One

B yearn; nearby
L utter; turtle
I agent; eating
N cease; seance
K ovine; invoke

Group Two

Q mouse; mosque
U typed; deputy
A curse; saucer
S peace; escape
H slice; chisel

Group Three

C angel; glance
R omens; sermon
Y gains; saying
P image; magpie
T field; lifted

Group Four

M alias; salami
A sorry; rosary
I snoop; poison
Z dingo; dozing
E thigh; height

Group Five

D steel; eldest
E choir; heroic
F beryl; belfry
O crane; cornea
G infer; fringe

Think Fast Quiz 11

1. The word "only" should be circled.
2. This blank should be empty.
3. MANE
4.

S	T	E	W
L	A	V	A
E	X	I	T
W	I	L	T

5. 1300
6. touchdown
7.
8. undo, unit, unto
9. No
10. Yes
11. The 2, 4, and 9 of hearts should be circled.
12. Circle pretzel. (It's from Germany.)
13. No
14. Twenty-four
15. The word underline appears twice in the sentence; both should be underlined.
16. END

Letter Insertion Quiz 2

Score one point for each correct letter. Add one point for every full minute early that you finished.

Group One
M STOR(M)Y
I HERO(I)N
X FLE(X)ES

Group Two
B STA(B)LE
I MA(I)NLY
K S(K)EWER
E B(E)ACON

Group Three
D MIL(D)ER
W BRE(W)ED
A BR(A)INY
R F(R)IGHT
F BERE(F)T

Group Four
P EX(P)ERT
Y G(Y)RATE
T NA(T)IVE
H BUS(H)ES
O METE(O)R
N PRI(N)CE

Group Five
S RE(S)IGN
Q FA(Q)IRS
U QUE(U)ER
E CR(E)ATE
L C(L)AUSE
C INSE(C)T
H T(H)READ

Ratings:
25+: Wow! This is an amazing letter-insertion score!
21-24: Excellent! You were almost letter-perfect!
17-20: Very good! Most of the letters fell into place.
Less than 17: You slipped a bit in slipping in letters.

Think Fast Quiz 12

1. The D in the word "third" should be underlined.
2. ILLEGAL
3. Yes
4. 16 cubes
5. This blank should be empty.
6. 31 cupcakes
7. Any 2 of: crypt, glyph, psych, tryst
8. BANJO
9. 38
10. Two
11. Ten
12. Circle "appeases."
13. Aquarius
14. This space should be blank.
15. Done

Score one point for each complete and correct answer. The maximum score is 15.
Ratings:
15: Amazing! You have an outstanding ability to think clearly under pressure.
13-14: Excellent! You kept focused throughout a tough challenge.
10-12: Very good! You probably keep on top of things both at work and at home.
7-9: OK. You solved several puzzles, but may have tripped up on others because of time pressures.
4-6: Fair. Some of this quiz's instructions were too tricky for you.
0-3: This type of timed test may not be your strong suit.

Scramble Up Quiz 4

Score one point for each correct letter. Add one point for every full minute early that you finished.

Group One

B cries; scribe
A otter; rotate
Y acorn; crayon
O craft; factor
U again; iguana

Group Two

C moist; sitcom
R stein; insert
I treat; attire
M eases; sesame
P dries; spider

Group Three

F minor; inform
L cigar; garlic
A cello; locale
K tries; strike
Y store; oyster

Group Four

U foams; famous
N image; enigma
W north; thrown
E tally; lately
D apron; pardon

Group Five

G nicer; cringe
H alien; inhale
O tried; editor
S thief; fetish
T canoe; octane

Ratings:
25+: Wow! You added a little something extra to your solving!
21-24: Excellent! Practically flawless in the mix.
17-20: Very good! You found many of the anagrams.
Less than 17: Well, you were scrambling.

Think Fast Quiz 13

1. K
2. JUICE
3. Thursday
4. 15 triangles
5. The square should be empty, and the next blank should contain the current year.
6. 250 (NOT 100)
7. 16 hyphens
8. Nine
9. 10
10. Oil, nil, nip, rip, rig (other answers are possible)
11. No
12. Circle SCRAM
13. Three
14. Brazil, Israel, Portugal (other answers are possible)
15. STOP

Score one point for each complete and correct answer. The maximum score is 15.
Ratings:
15: Amazing! You have an outstanding ability to think clearly under pressure.
13-14: Excellent! You kept focused throughout a tough challenge.
10-12: Very good! You probably keep on top of things both at work and at home.
7-9: OK. You solved several puzzles, but may have tripped up on others because of time pressures.
4-6: Fair. Some of this quiz's instructions were too tricky for you.
0-3: This type of timed test may not be your strong suit.

Brain Stretchers Quiz 4

Score one point for each answer in the correct blank. Add one point for every full minute early that you finished.

Group One

C House coat
E Off ice
B
A A mount
D In tent

Group Two

D
A
E Incan descent
B For king
C Not iced

Group Three

E Bass I net
D Subs ample
A
C
B

Group Four

B
C End anger
D
E He-brides
A

Group Five

D To a sty
A
B
E A band on
C Be a ten

Ratings:
25+: Wow! Your brain is quite nimble.
21-24: Excellent! Your ability to spot relationships is well-developed.
17-20: Very good! Your brain is alive and kicking.
13-16: Good. You thought your way through several pairings.
Less than 13: Your brain may need a kick-start!